Getting to Gran's

Written by
Jill Atkins

Illustrated by
Elisa Patrissi

Clare, Karl and Bear got up at half-past seven. It was the day of Gran's birthday party.

"I love Gran," said Clare.

"Me too," said Bear.

"What shall I wear?" asked Clare.

"Dungarees?" said Mum.

They rushed to the car and got in. Mum turned the key. Nothing!

"Oh no! Flat battery!" she cried.

"Let's go by train," said Clare. "I like going on trains."

"Me too," said Bear.

They walked to the train. Mum paid the fare as the train came in.

"Take care you don't fall," said Mum.

They all piled in and sat down.

They looked out of the window as the train left town.

"I'm so excited!" exclaimed Karl.

"Me too," said Bear.

Soon, the train slowed down and stopped.

"This train stops here," the announcer said over the speaker. "A tree has fallen on the line. All passengers must get off."

Clare looked across the road.

"There is a bus," she said. "Let's go on that. I rather like buses."

"Me too," said Bear.

They ran to the bus. Clare was first to climb on.

She walked to the back.

"Shall we share a seat?" she asked Karl.

The driver started the bus. They drove along main roads and narrow lanes. They stopped in a town square.

"This is where we stop," said the driver. "Everyone off, please!"

"What shall we do now?" asked Karl.

"Look!" shouted Clare. "There's a cab."

They all piled into the cab.

"This is my first ride in a cab," said Karl.

"Me too," said Bear.

Then, clunk, clunk! The cab broke down.

"Quick!" called Mum. "Everyone out!"

They stood at the side of the road.

"This is getting silly!" cried Karl. "We will never get to Gran's!"

"Calm down," said Mum. "It will be fine."

At that moment, Clare spotted some bikes in a rack.

"Look!" she shouted. "Bikes for hire! I like to ride a bike."

"Me too," said Bear.

Mum paid for bikes and helmets. Karl and Clare had their own bikes. Bear sat behind Mum.

A signpost pointed to Gran's town.

"Let's go!" said Clare, as she began to pedal.

But then there was a hissing sound. Karl stopped.

"Look at my wheel!" he yelled. "I have a puncture."

"We'll have to walk with the bikes," said Clare.

Just then, it started to rain. Soon they were all soaked. Splash! Dirty water sprayed all over them.

At last, they reached Gran's.

"Come in," she laughed. "I'll find some things for you to wear."

When they joined the party, everyone grinned.

"I forgot to tell you all," said Gran. "It's a fancy dress party!"